The Glenmore Sessions

Joseph Fulkerson

Joseph Fulkerson

Fulkerson2693@gmail.com
Josephfulkerson.com

The Glenmore Sessions/Joseph Fulkerson

ISBN:9781091695849
IndependentlyPublished

DEDICATION

To the late-nighters, the all-nighters, the roughnecks, and all keepers of the flame.

v

The Glenmore Sessions

Joseph Fulkerson

TABLE OF CONTENTS

ACKNOWLEDGMENTS

I would like to thank the editors of the following journals in which these poems in one form or another were published: "The Glenmore Sessions"-Verbatim issue #1, "21 Grams"-Pegasus Spring 2019, "The Curmudgeon"-Pegasus summer 2019, "We, the Chosen Leftovers"-The Esthetic Apostle December 2018

21 Grams

Lately I've been thinking about my own
mortality and just how fragile life can be.

They claim that at the time of death,
when your soul leaves your body,
you lose twenty-one grams of weight.

If we're counting, that's eight pennies.
Or fifteen paper clips if you will.
That's nineteen jelly beans.
Better yet, one hundred raindrops
on a chilly autumn morning.

It troubles me to think that everything that
makes us unique carries so little weight.
It seems so insignificant.

When I die, I want the sun to supernova
and the earth to spin off its axis.
I want the oceans to be at rest
so the tide never comes back in.

When I leave this earth, I want people
to wonder how they could ever
go on in my absence.
Twenty-one grams isn't enough.
My soul feels so much heavier than that.

The Free Spirit

As she danced,
the whole world danced with her,
swirling around in step
with every movement she made,
with every flit of her hair,
every stolen glance.

She danced to remember,
she danced to forget.
She danced so she would live again,
so she could believe again.

She danced because she had to,
it was in her and if she didn't
it would come bursting out of her
like an atom bomb,
her own personal Hiroshima.

As I watched, I was surprised, aroused,
confounded, captivated...
For with each movement of her body
and twirl of her hair
she was born anew.

The Pretender

Oh great pretender,
you have everyone fooled.
Everyone that is, but me.
I see through your facade.
You can't blend in
no matter how hard you try.
You put on your hat
or that uniform,
and you may wear them for a while
but none of them fit,
none of them feel like you.

Oh great pretender,
how foolish you are
to think that I don't know your secret.
Longing to be where you belong,
what a tragic waste of potential
that lays at your feet.

Oh great pretender,
you must take heed
post haste
don't waste another day
knowing
knowing
knowing
that the biggest catastrophe
in your life was the day you
decided to settle for second best

at best, giving up on blazing your
own path, creating your own truth,
resigning yourself to hem the inseam
of another man's vision.

In the Shadows

I see God waiting in the
shadows, as a child would.
I feel his presence
in the pause between breaths,
the breaks between sets.
He seems to be waiting for me
to acknowledge him,
but I can't bring myself to do it
so, there he stays.

Unremarkable

We are the unremarkable generation,
masters of mediocrity.
Starved for truth and craving beauty,
we perform our dance
until we break, or something breaks in us
tumbling down to the scorched earth,
taking shallow roots in our misery.

We stumble around in the darkness,
groping and clawing at shapes and
silhouettes, gasping out last breaths
with collapsed lungs,
returning to the uterine tomb
of our ancestors,
until that time when each of us
must give account
for burning ourselves
on the altars of compromise.

Adults Should Get Snow Days

The sunlight feels so good
standing in front of the glass door,
although it won't last.
It's five degrees outside,
there's snow on the ground
that won't go away and
the house still smells like pizza.
My hands are so dry.
I like the word marmalade,
it sounds fun rolling off my tongue.

Borderland

The persistent gaze
of the outlander-
burnt sienna landscape,
charcoal sunset.
He sits in silence
the scope of his gun
trained on the horizon,
surveying his next move
towards the borderlands.

Déjà vu

It feels so strange to me
sitting in this chair.
I've sat here so many times
with the same thoughts,
had the same conversations
with myself,
trying to find my way
through this muck pile I call life.

He died of an enlarged cerebral cortex
and an engorged sense of discontent,
matched only by his inability
to take a chance on his life.

Fallout

A boy lives a thousand lives
as a pirate, ninja, or superhero.

A girl pushes a stroller
and plays dress up.

A man smells of smeared dirt
and sweat glands.

A woman walks briskly towards
the errands of the day.

All a result of the fallout
that day in the Garden.

Friction

Racism is taught
from the hearts of scared people.

Skepticism is learned
from countless disappointments.

Sarcasm is expressed
through world-weary lips.

Love is created
from the friction of two hearts
joining together to form one
singular heartbeat.

A Spark

Just a spark is all it takes.
A glint of sunlight
off a reflective surface,
friction created by two rocks
to ignite a firestorm
that will consume whole forests,
subdivisions full of homes,
towns and businesses
churches and schools
forever changing the landscape.

The Curmudgeon

I'm not satisfied
unless it's raining.
I'm talking torrential downpour,
broken levee kind of rain.

I'm not happy
until the verdict is in:
capital murder in the first,
no possibility of parole.

I'm not worried
until the market has crashed,
the bubble has burst wide,
and the bottom has
fallen out of it all.

I'm unable to empathize
with angry crowds gathered
to protest my right to use
the family bathroom at Target alone.

I won't be swayed
by your ability
to conjugate full sentences
and I am unavailable
for comment.

Primal

The primal howl of a man
who's given up on giving in
to the daily ritual of cutting one's flesh
and letting the blood flow like a river,
overflowing its banks in the springtime
and releasing the scream
of legions of frustrated souls,
and a thousand hungry wolves
fighting over the carcass of a solitary deer.

The Glenmore Sessions

All my friends reside within
the urban jungle of my mind-
the deep thinker
the free spirit
the thrifty penny salesman
the college professor,
professing his love for
all things Tarantino.

Imagine me in a world
that can't exist without you in it,
and that would come close to
explaining how I feel about wintertime.
The time between sunrise and sunset
is squandered away most days
on work and regret.

I want to dive headlong into the oceans
that lie within your beautiful blue eyes.
If I drown it will have been for a good
cause. If I live, it'll be on my own terms.

Dreams of a Sequoia

My soul is old
hundreds, maybe
thousands of years old.
There's no way of knowing
unless you cut me open
and count the rings.

Ode to Autumn

A cold breeze blows
filling the air with
the damp smell
of decaying leaves,
the end of a heat wave
the beginning of a cool down,
the crunching sound of grass
shocked by the first frost,
fog-filled cornfields welcoming dusk,
the uneasy feeling of loss
lingers in the air
like a bird, wings extended
letting the Jetstream
do all the work.

It hovers over my world
as a reminder that
the book is closing
on another year,
it whispers in my ear
winter is coming.
The wind and the sleet
and the snow
will conspire
to envelope me
in a fortress of precipitation
forcing me to wait,
with arms folded
for the daffodils to return

and life to begin anew.

Adventures in Insomnia

My head in the clouds,
my feet taking me to places
unknown, unknowingly putting me
in dangerous or uncomfortable circumstances,
desperately seeking comfort or some reprieve
from the monotony of my heartbeat,
counting my breaths in multiples of four
until my face goes numb and my eyes
roll in their sockets, tucking my hands
under me while I sit, finally able to feel
something real, something tangible,
calmly biting my tongue until I feel
the bitter taste of copper spurt and hit the roof
of my mouth, satisfying my bloodlust and allowing
the sweet serenity of nothingness to wash over me
like a tsunami of infinite sleep.

It.

It cannot be taught
It cannot be bought,
It cannot be learned
or conjured up.
It cannot be passed down.

If you can't feel it,
all apologies.
If you don't have it,
you never will.

Frank

Hard apple cider for the soul
take a drink, they'll never know.
You'll flit your arms and dance about,
you'll laugh and sing and dance and shout.
It'll fill your mind with many things,
from visions of grandeur to angels' wings.
The nectar of the gods
you'll swear you've drank,
until you wake up in bed
next to your new friend Frank.

The Companionship of the Lonely

I am surrounded by people
daily, yet alone.
Throngs of people,
faceless wads of flesh
meandering from one great
attraction to the next,
stuffing their faces with endless
amounts of mindless entertainment,
never curbing their appetites
for the extravagant, the macabre.
It must be taboo to hold their
microscopic attention spans
for mere moments.

My Process

Write write
write rewrite,
rework
rewrite
write write write write
rework, write

rewrite
write write
write write,
write
write
write rewrite,
trash

If You Look for Me, Don't Use Google Maps

I dwell on the outskirts of sanity,
just past normal, take a left at the first stoplight.
Continue until you reach a fork in the road.
If you think you should go left, go right instead.
Keep going until you start second guessing yourself.

When you feel like you should stop and ask for directions,
take an immediate right onto the first black-topped
one lane road and continue from there until you come
to a four way stop.

Plow right through the intersection with your eyes closed.
When you open your eyes, slam on the emergency brake
and drift onto the second gravel road on the left.
Take that gravel road all the way to the horizon,
past the fields ravaged by years of harvesting
without rest, past the old barn in the throes of being
repossessed by mother nature,
past the condemned meth lab.

Take that road all the way to the horizon.

If you're lucky, you just might catch
a glimpse of me in my natural habitat
amongst the enlightened souls
where we are free to be.

Sonic Youth

I am a child of the 90's,
the decade of change
Nintendo and chocolate Yoo-hoos,
sleepovers with friends,
church revivals and field trips
to the ice rink with our homeschool group.

When the scariest things were getting caught
watching episodes of Beavis and Butthead,
Ren & Stimpy and Singled out.

When the President didn't inhale
and his intern didn't swallow.
O.J.'s gloves didn't fit right
and Tupac was dreaming of California.

I'll see you at the crossroads, Easy E...

Nirvana Unplugged and Stone Temple Pilot's
albums were the soundtrack of a summer.

*Black hole sun, won't you come
and wash away the rain...*

When Picard was Captain of the Starship Enterprise.

"Oh Captain, my Captain!"

When Pulp Fiction and Seven blew my freaking mind.
Tarantino is a god of cinema.

That time I professed my love with spray paint
under the old blue bridge and my truck
got hung up in the mud trying to leave.

Those nights I climbed ever so quietly into
my girlfriend's bedroom window to sneak a peek.
When driving Steve's baby blue 64' Impala
up and down Frederica Street on a Friday
night was the thing to do.

That time we drank all his brother's whiskey
and ran headlong into the summer night
like madmen. He got so mad when we watered
it down to cover our tracks.

That night we met in Applebee's parking lot to fight
and I ended up kicking our friendship's ass.

What I'm trying to say is
I want to worry like the birds,
in other words, not at all.

I wish I could go back to the time
before I knew the world was
a dark and broken place,
where everything was
a Frank Sinatra song,

when everything was beautiful
and nothing hurt.

Query #1

Can you find everything you need
in the eyes of one woman?
Can you find total fulfillment
in her embrace?

I've been lost in the gaze
of a thousand pair of eyes,
mesmerized by every color imaginable,
falling time and time again
looking into the light
searching for that elusive spark.

Did I see it? Was it there?
I'm not sure.

What should we do?
Is it worth the risk?
The answer to all of those
questions is probably not.

To Alisa

She was an energy burst,
full of life and lust and zeal
to love with all her heart.

She was destined and determined
to slay the hearts of men
and boys alike.

The Girl from Jeffersonville

I met a girl with a beautiful face,
blonde hair and fire in her eyes.
She spoke of life and love
in such a contagious manner
that it burst out of every
pore on her body.

She's a sunspot, a solar flare,
the remnants of a star
that had reached supernova.
Her intelligence was apparent
with each turn of the phrase.
Her body language enticing
me to become one with her.
Her eyes, her lips, her mannerisms
revealing the truth she had hidden
for so long.

She moved me to embrace
every breath of every day
as if it was my last.

Springsteen

It's such a cliché, I know
to have a memory of a song
that is about the very subject
of songs having the ability to
transport us to a time and place
that was etched into our consciousness,
like some mysterious tattoo artist
imprinting a cherry on an ankle,
or a name like Tracy or Angela
across some poor soul's chest.

It's so old hat to say that we were alive
that brisk night in January at the Eric Church
concert, you with your short dress and cowboy
boots, me wearing my plaid shirt and that
soon to be broken heart on my sleeve.
You were standing while everyone else
sat, arms stretched out and beer in hand
swaying in sync with the singer's crooning voice.

I know what you're thinking, and I've since come
to my senses, yet up to that moment I'd never felt
so alive considering we succeeded in stopping
or at least slowing time down to our speed
and forever making that night, that moment ours.

Illogical Patterns

Life consists of illogical patterns.
Cycles of pain and bliss,
neither balanced nor fair
yet equally instrumental
in developing the silhouette
of the soul.

Untitled #4

We lay awake pondering
the mysteries of the stars
and jazz,
drunk on the possibilities
of what lie ahead of us.

Mended

You know that broken heart?
The one you've been meticulously
piecing back together since the last time?
Let me help you with that. I've been working
on mine for a while now, and I think
I'm getting the hang of it.

Moonlight Serenade

Everything eventually fades to black,
even the beloved ones
with fingers intertwined,
and bodies writhing in orgasmic elation
are no longer keepers
of the forbidden promises,
whispered long into the morning,
repeated a million times
into unworthy or ubiquitous ear canals,
bounding from rooftop to steeplechase
to moss covered stumps,
shrouded by the secret sanctuary
of forgotten hideaways.

Carnal desire makes
throbbing fools out of all
who indulge in the lifelong ballet
of the *damned if you don't* crowd.

Queen of Broken Hearts

She's painted on the outside
but empty, cracked
and undone on the inside.
She's the queen of hearts,
or more appropriately
the queen of broken hearts.

A Dream

I dreamt that you were still here,
that you still loved me,
that we were still happy,
that I hadn't messed up yet.

Desolation

I stand defiant
chest out
chin up
spine rigid.
I stare into the eyes
of the abyss
and laugh.
I yell my guts out.
I dare the loneliness
to suck me in.
I invite the succubus
with the barbed wire tongue
to rip out my heart,
ravish my mind
and damn my soul into oblivion.

I am not afraid of the darkness.

Outside the Nuclear Safe Zone the Flowers Are Absolutely Radiant!

I need to know I still exist somewhere
between the lines of your hands
and the soles of your feet.

The morning after can be lonely,
that long walk back to the bar
where I left my truck and
stumbled into a cab,
stumbling towards another
last night with you,
the comfort of lying next to you,
pretending we didn't disembowel
each other trying to say goodbye,
leaving a trail of tears like bread crumbs,
leading to the safe place we drug our
hemorrhaging bodies to recover
from our near fatal encounter.

I need to know you still think about
what might have been.
I need to know you look at the stars
differently because of us.
I need to know the scars on your body
are still too tender to the touch,
that you still hold your breath
when you hear our song,
that you still close your eyes when you pass

by those places that were white-hot
seared into your memories.
Say it, even if it's untrue.

Saturday Evening at Smother's Park

Do you remember that spot in the park
by the swings, where we met to say
goodbye one more time?
Do you remember that the band
was playing our song?

Do you remember the dance that we shared?
The last point of physical contact we would ever have?

Do you remember how we couldn't
look into each other's eyes for fear
of seeing something worth the heartache
and the pain we caused each other?

Do you remember how I looked standing there
in the dark, leaning against the railing,
surveying the abyss before me?
When you walked away from me that night
did you take one last look?

As I stand here tonight in this same
exact spot, I can feel it all.
I can hear the hesitation in our voices.
I can feel the longing to be in each other's arms.
They say if it's true love it will last.
Time will erase all the doubts away, right?

Query #2

What does depression look like?
Does it look like a sink full of dishes,
an unkempt house,
an overgrown yard?

What does it feel like?
A suffocating weight lying on your chest?
Deep sadness lingering in an empty house?
Silence in my kid's bedrooms,
where there should be noise
and commotion
and signs of life?

What does depression sound like?
The splashing of tears soaking
the living room carpet?

What does it smell like?
Stale air circulating endlessly
in the dungeon of my mind?

What does it taste like?
Like a heated-up TV dinner?
A bowl of ramen noodles?

Is this depression?
How is one to know?

Not Likely

Such is our lot in life,
to love and be loved,
to need and be needed,
to fuck and be fucked by,
to hurt and be hurt,
to hate and to be loathed,
to remember and be reminded
of all the missed opportunities
and failures that might have been
had we been different people,
lives intersecting
at different times,
in different places.
Is it better to have loved and lost?
Not likely.

Talking Scars

"Just know that someone out there loves you,"
she said.

What am I supposed to do with that?
Will that keep me from freezing to death
in the blizzard of my own desire?

Will it provide me with a cup of water
in the desert of my loneliness?

Will it give me resolve in the congregation
of my enemies?

Can it sustain me into my latter years
when my mind is eaten by dementia?

Will it be my *get out of jail free* card
when I need it most?

I have lost precious sight and countless
years pondering the words and phrases
carelessly cast at me.

"It was a pleasure to have met you"
 and
"I'm a better man because of you," I said.
Then she said, "Those are just the scars talking."

Dawn

I find myself thinking of you
from time to time,
but not as often as I used to
and with smaller effects
on my soul.

I do think I've turned a corner,
my heart is mending,
my spirit is raising,
the dawn of a new day is coming
if I can just hold out a little longer.

Night Shift at the Dam

One and a half inch
rigid metallic conduit
bend a back-to-back 90
with a six-inch kicker
on the triple-nickel
we need a ten-inch offset
starting at twenty-four inches
from the end of the pipe,
cut and rethread the pipe
with the help of a *porta pony*
making sure to file away
the burr after the cut.

My tool buddy climbs down
the shaft of the turbine
to layout the next run
with his angle finder
his tape measure,
and his head filled
with numbers,
angles and formulas.
Take-up and gain must be factored in
as well as the direction the bends will take
on their way down to the cable tray.

He calls out the measurements
from the dark, I write them down and visualize
the routing it will take to conform
to the inward parts of the shaft down

to the destination below. As he climbs back up
I mark and ready the pipe to be shaped
into the image we come up with.
Piece by piece is bent and cut to fit
and lowered into the abyss
to be assembled and installed
in accordance with the standards set
by those who blazed the trail before us.
It takes precision, patience, and skill
to visualize the flow of pipe.

We must utilize all our combined
experience as technique, tradition
and technology unite to create
the mindset of tomorrow's craftsman.

We, the Chosen Leftovers

Wave upon wave of thick ash
and smoldering brick raining down,
showering the navel gazers
and nexus glimpsers alike.
I see the silhouette of a demigod
looking down with disdain on us peasants.

A pyromaniac's wet dream,
liquid fire for the heathens,
quantum breakup in the cosmos.
The axis of evil has a rotating cast of characters
and we are the host country for the yearly festivities.

If you'll please direct your attention to the choir director
with the Sam's Club haircut, we can begin the show.

The preacher grabbed us while the music
played and took us to the back of the sanctuary.
He said with bloodshot eyes, if we didn't stop talking
he was going to bust our asses, plural.
We walked back to our seats
as he walked back to the front.
He continued to worship his Lord and Savior,
while we re-evaluated our understanding
of organized religion.

We all fall for something,
it's a zero-sum game we're playing now.
No rest for the wicked, but the saints

are having the time of their lives, aren't they?
In the end, Saddam Hussein was found cowering in a
bunker.
Where will you be when the world ends?
The Rapture will occur,
and cause everyone's clothes to fall off
like an aphrodisiac, and we'll be left with the
hand-me-downs.

Meet me in the city square on the day of reckoning.
I'll be the one with the trash bag full of clothes,
dancing barefoot in the fountain.

Will the circle be unbroken?
The real question is will it become some other
shape in the process, or will it
have any discernable shape at all.

What if predestination is a lie
passed down to us from our ancestors
to keep us from asking too many questions?

We live, we die,
we fail, we cry
and we struggle for what?

Mediocrity is really spelled C-O-N-F-O-R-M-I-T-Y.
We're reading from the holy book: chapter 7
starting with verse 3. The gospel according to whom?

God gave us this planet
and now he's trying to evict us,
but as tenants we have rights-
He must give us thirty days of notice
before he unleashes the Beast
and hastens the Apocalypse.

3 Questions for a Future Iteration of Myself

Me: How do I continue to do something I hate
day in and day out? Will I ever get away from
this sense of restlessness and unfulfilledness?

Future self: Is unfulfilledness even a real word?
Anyways, it's not about a different job per se,
but a better understanding of our place in the universe.
We all have a purpose, and part of that purpose is
figuring it out.

Me: Unfulfillment. That's what I meant.

Future self: That makes more sense.

Me: In your opinion, does love last?

Future self: Love. Wow you went there. Okay,
how do I put this, you fall in and out of love with
various people at various times. You may not be able
to choose who you love, but you can choose who you continue
to love and be committed to. Commitment is love in action.

Me: What about God? We were raised to believe in him, the
bible, and all that Sunday school stuff. Do you still believe?

Future self: Yes of course! Jesus came back a while ago
and revealed himself to the whole earth. He's actually
pretty cool and he has a great sense of humor. I guess you'd
have to after this long...

Me: Wait, what?! Are you kidding Me? That's great!

Future self: Oh yeah it was until the Antichrist
showed up. Jesus recruited a holy army and we had
to fight in the "war to end all wars." A lot of people died.

Me: ...

Come on

She said come on
I said let's go
she said hold on
I said what for?
She said I'm coming
I said I'm going
she said we're leaving
I said I'm gone.

She said you're always gone
when I'm around.

I said I'm always here
while you're away.
Always away from
where I want to be,
I told her.

Perhaps, she said
but never on time
for dinner.

Like Moths to a Flame

We are two moths in the darkness
drawn to the same orange glow of light.
I think it's just that simple,
that's how people meet.
Running from the darkness toward the light,
we bump up against those seeking similar reprieve.

His Side

"For what I've been through I'm surprised
I have any hope at all," he said. Even as the
words slipped off his tongue he felt it fade a little more.

He wanted to step once again into the darkness
like he had done so many times before. He knew it
was the right thing to do, yet the sunshine poured
out from her with a radiance so pure and all encompassing
it compelled him to stay and be consumed by it.

For the first time he felt alive. For the first time
he was open to the possibility of witnessing the birth
of love in its purest form.

From Time to Time

You may have to remind me,
from time to time
to breathe when I am around you.

A Pound of Flesh

Welcome all followers of the Worm
to the festival of the aborted ones,
the soft spot of society requests
your presence at the head of the table,
in the hollowed out remains of a tortoiseshell.

From the umbilical womb of the earth
comes forth the blood-tinged youth,
tomorrow's forgotten children,
bastard reminders of a tryst long past.

I go to sleep every night
in a spaceship built with tinker toys.
Searing a path through the firmament
I ascend to the heights of the gods,
collecting cosmic dust on my way to
the total annihilation of every celestial
body that stands in my way.

I will seek court with the daughters of Zeus
and Mnemosyne, carve out my pound of flesh
and toss it on the altar in an act of supreme
worship to the muse.

Her side

And in the end, she listened to her heart,
for it was the only one she could trust
to tell her the truth.

My Companions

I'm left all alone with my demons.
I have made my peace with them
and they've settled for me.

In times like these
they are my only companions,
my friends, my confidants,
and in return I don't exorcise them.

Birds and Bees

Life is a lot like sex. It's full of ups and downs,
ins and outs. Sometimes you're getting screwed,
other times you're doing the screwing.
Often it feels like you're putting in
more than you're getting out.
It's hot, messy, and almost too overwhelming to process.
Yet time after time we come back for more.
Because honestly, what else is there?

Necromancer

You dance in my dreams,
hallucinations of our hopes and dreams haunt me.
Remorse for what once was
that will never be again.
Tears fall unaccounted for in isolation
as I wait for the return to the past.
The glory days of yesteryear taken for granted,
never understanding the absolute fragility
and fleeting nature of it all.
The streets of my soul are littered
with the corpses of yesterday's promises.
The plans laid out for our future abandoned,
aborted.
evacuated.

What do I do with the feelings of loss
that are so prevalent, so overwhelming
that I can't think, let alone speak
for fear that I might feel something real,
something tangible.
something reliable.
I miss you.
I love you.
I miss your smell,
I miss your taste,
I miss the feeling of you being near,
I miss the look you would give me
when you wanted me.
I'm sorry I didn't recognize the signs.

I'm sorry that I wasn't everything you wanted
me to be, everything that you needed me to be.
I'm sorry that I couldn't hold on.
I'm sorry that I was overwhelmed by the sheer magnitude
of the obstacles that prevented me from going on.
I tried. I tried so damn hard.
I wanted to work it out so much, that I couldn't dream
of anything else.
I'm a fool.
I am a failure in love.

Human

I've been called a liar, a cheater, a pervert, a saint.
I've been called a brother, a father, a friend, soulmate.
I've been called daddy, a lover, an instigator, an agitator,
an employee, a boss, a son.
I have been all of these to some and none to others,
yet not one of them define me.
I am a collage of good and bad choices, hard work,
and a lot of luck.
The very definition of what it is to be human.

Am I Beautiful?

She pointed out the imperfections in her beauty,
but all I could see was the beauty in her imperfections.

Girl, you are beautiful from the inside out.
Wars are waged for women such as yourself.
Men live and die for your affection
and your attention.
Life and death are within your gaze.
Your kisses are immobilizing, tantalizing
mesmerizing, life giving, sustaining.
Your favor is worth more than all the gold
ever mined from the belly of this earth.

You move the hearts of kings, toppling their kingdoms with
a mere glance.
You have captivated the expanses of my imagination
and become my muse.
I have willingly and gleefully given you my heart and soul,
caution thrown to the wind,
left to the gods
to sort out as they see fit.

Kissed the Heavens

I have kissed the heavens with prayers
for answers to the mystery
that surrounds my existence.
Forgive me Father, for I have sinned.
I dared to dream of more
than this meager existence.

Insomniac Nightmare

Don't wake us up from this nightmare.
We will swallow our amnesia pills,
folding our hands into triangles.

We will rehabilitate ourselves,
or jump the shark into oblivion,
laying down beside our ancestors
to never again trust the uncertainties
of our youth.

The Spectator

I'm a fly on the wall,
watching life pass me by.
I'm always here, but few know it.

I'm a wallflower, blending into the background.
Banished to the outskirts of the social circles,
I sit and watch the habits of the masses,
studying their mannerisms,
developing charts and graphs,
theories and pie charts.

I'm a wild life photographer,
lying belly down in the tall
grasses of the Sahara waiting
for that perfect snapshot.

I'm a honey bee buzzing
from meadow to flower
to the can of diet coke in your hands,
straw pressed to your lips,
waiting impatiently to dip my
mouth into your saccharin sweetness.

To the Limit

I wanted to see how far I could go,
I wanted to know how long I could last.
I had to know my limitations,
pushing myself to the outer limits of sanity,
I crossed that line long ago.
I didn't even look back, the thought hadn't
occurred to me until now.

The Anatomy of a Poet

I think in poems
and speak in haiku.
I dream of rhyme, with
rhythm in my bones.
There's cadence in my step,
my movements in verse,
stanza and couplet.

The High Road

When you are hurt by someone,
especially someone you care for deeply,
it's very easy to want them to feel the hurt as well.
It's second nature even, to take the low road
of revenge and vindictiveness.

Confucius said, "Before you embark on a journey of revenge,
dig two graves." Now, I believe that can be taken two ways.
You can lose your life in the literal sense of the word; you
will die.

Yet I also believe he was alluding to the death of the soul.
Once you go down that road, there is no coming back.
It will change you. You will stoop down and become
something that you're not, and that will doom you.

So I implore you, take the high road of forgiveness.
It is a rocky, uneven path uphill the entire way,
but it is the only road to enlightenment.

Supernova

There is a sunburst in my soul that must escape.
It's burning so hot and bright, if I don't
release it, it will scorch my insides,
all of me consumed in a supernova
blast that could destroy the universe
as we know it.

The Dragon

The dragon looms heavy over my conscience,
ever present, ever closer
his breath hot with sulfur,
clawing his way up my throat,
his mouth becoming my own,
his words becoming my words,
my tongue splitting into bifurcated twins.
He seeks out the woman with child,
he must consume it and become one with its essence.
He must ensure the bloodline continues no further.

The Silent Suck

It's funny how accustomed you get
to the little things in a relationship.
The things you may take for granted
on a day to day basis,
things you didn't realize meant so much
to you until they're no longer there.
A text message, a phone call,
the presence of another,
even just the general contentment that someone
is there for you, will be there for you.
Knowing that when you get home they'll be there,
or you'll see them or talk to them soon.

A person is aware of these things after they're gone,
leaving only a small void in its wake.
Sometimes it's the small things that cause the most pain.
You may not miss the person in particular,
but you miss the thought of someone caring,
of someone being there for you.

In the dead of night, when you wake up and there's nothing
but the silent suck of darkness to keep you company, it
would be comforting to know that someone, somewhere is
thinking of you.

Query #3

What if he had been more like the others?
Would they have liked him more?
Would she have loved him?
Would she have stayed?
Would he have been happier?
Would he have taken his own life?
Would you have noticed?

What if she had been more like the others?
Would she have been liked more and
in turn lived a happier life?
Would he have loved her and stayed?
Would it have prevented her
from taking her life?
Would you have even noticed?

If I had been more like the others,
everyone would have liked me.
She would have loved me more,
and would've stayed.
I, no doubt would've been happier,
I wouldn't have dreamt of taking my life.
You'd never known any different.

March 13, 2014

Standing on the beach,
watching the waves crash upon the shore,
I can't help but feel the pull of the receding waves.
As each wave folds back into itself,
I want to go with it.
I want to follow it into to the deep recesses of the sea,
discovering all its mysteries,
learning its rhythm and ride its currents
down to the belly of the fish
to forget and be forgotten.

Love is a Four-Letter Word

I saw colors and felt electricity
when you told me that you loved me.
I heard the heartbeat of a thousand lovers
in your voice, the flutter of thousands of dove wings.
Fireworks went off in my brain
and my vision blurred.
Your love for me was like the completion of a novel
I have been writing my entire life.
Hearing you say the words "I love you"
was like remembering the lyrics to a song
that I haven't heard in years.

So, if you're going to break my heart,
make sure you destroy it so completely
that no one can put it back together again.

Divots of the Soul

The reverberations of our love echoes into oblivion,
making its long trek into the negative spaces
between what was and what could have been.
Like divinations of the past, the highs and the lows
make divots in my soul, scraping away the deposits
that have clung to my insides,
leaving only longing and the absence of fire
which I guess would be cold or ice.
The long, lanky fingers of death reach down and deposit
morsels of regret and remorse which sow seeds
of discontent and longing for love once more.

I don't want to need someone to complete
the puzzle in my heart,
but there are pieces missing
and I'm not sure where they are.

My hope is someone, somewhere is holding them tightly.
That they take them out occasionally
and examine them, wondering,
fantasizing about who they belong to.

Inconsequential

Love stinks.
Everything about it is inconsequential.
None of it matters in the grand scheme of things.
In the *Master Plan*
it is but a flash in the pan,
a blip on the radar,
a pin prick on the thumb of the Almighty.
The sum of its parts equal less than nothing.

A sparrow falls,
a storm ravaged town picks up the pieces,
a lonely soul wanders to the edge of the dimly lit bridge,
rain cascading down on the homeless, the hopeless
she lay in bed listless,
he beside her helpless, loveless.

The ever changing, consistently disappointing,
ruthless nature of love ceases to exist in the spaces
of my heart, abandoned under the cover of darkness,
debris scattered about the corridors,
hinting of life long gone.

Codependent

When I see her face,
the radiation kills every cell in me.
When I hear her voice,
my spine splinters under the weight
of every enunciated syllable.

I know I don't need her,
but I want to need her
and she needs me to need her
just as much.

Invocation of the Muse

O muse, how doth thou awaken me!
You breathe upon the coals of inspiration,
causing the smoldering secrets of the universe to ignite,
giving birth to the spark of creativity that defines me
that drives me, that keep the hounds of hell at bay,
if only for mere moments,
that I may write these words.

Mosaic of Heartbreak

My heart breaks into a hundred pieces.
Then, in the fires of our passion
is fused back together.
A mosaic of a thousand heartaches
joined together just to be broken again.

Instead

Instead of building a house, I'll tear yours down.
Instead of investing my money,
I'll spend it all and rob you at knife point.
Instead of creating an environment conducive
of creativity and spiritual exploration,
I'll fill mine with self-loathing, doubt and regret.
Short attention spans required.

Apparition

She's an apparition. She haunts me.
So much soul contained in one fleeting glance.
It makes my heart ache to the core of every chamber.
The muscle pumps and the blood flows in unison
with the tears.
A dull ache fills the expanses of my soul
like noxious gas chamber fumes.
I am addicted to the poison on her lips.
She wrapped her barbed tongue
around mine and I was no longer in control.

The bleakness of my outcome even worried
the purveyor of my iniquities. Satan himself
made excuses for my behavior,
downplaying the condition of my mortal soul.
"This soul belongs in heaven with the other hypocritical
social elitist conservative, like-minded succubus.
They deserve every fluffy cloud enema that they get,"
he says.

You call me cynical, outrageous, even blasphemous.
You'll see. Give it time to germinate.
Give it time to sow its seed across the fields
of your dreams.
It will populate the vast expanses of your future
memories into infinity.

Thy kingdom come thy will be done,
regardless of my objections.

Query #4

If misery loves company,
does that mean that love's company is miserable?
Maybe misery is love's plus-one.
Does that mean love wants to be associated with it?
No, he's just here for the free booze.

Mind Your Business

I don't exactly have all the answers, but I have some.
I don't know everything, but I know enough to get by.
I may not have the most money, but I am the richest man.
you might have a problem with me, but I like you just fine.
You may not like my outlook on life.
You may have a problem with my attitude.
You may not like the way I raise my kids.
You may not like my work ethic,
the way I prioritize my life,
the food I choose to eat,
the way I pay my bills,
the music I listen to,
my workout routine,
my religion
my voice
my face.

But none of that matters.
None of it makes a bit of difference
in the long run
or the short term.
It's my life.
Not yours,
mine.

And I will spark and shine
stumble and fall,
break out and find success.
I will yell and scream

at the top of my lungs,
in the deepest darkest cave,
or the peak of the tallest mountain.

I will live my life
assured and unassuming
steadily, happily
until my dying breath,
unashamed that it didn't meet your criteria,
regretting only having not lived
according to the tempo
of my own soul.

 Joseph Fulkerson is a writer of poetry and haiku. His work has been published in numerous print and online journals. He currently resides in Owensboro, Kentucky. The Glenmore Sessions is his first collection of poetry spanning 2014 to 2018.

Made in the USA
San Bernardino, CA
20 July 2020

75791827R00063